FAMILIES

Popcorn

My Dad

Katie Dicker

WAYLAND

Explore the world with **Popcorn** - your complete first non-fiction library.

Look out for more titles in the Popcorn range. All books have the same format of simple text and striking images. Text is carefully matched to the pictures to help readers to identify and understand key vocabulary.
www.waylandbooks.co.uk/popcorn

First published in 2010 by Wayland
Copyright © Wayland 2010

Wayland
Hachette Children's Books
338 Euston Road
London NW1 3BH

Wayland Australia
Level 17/207 Kent Street
Sydney NSW 2000

Produced for Wayland by
White-Thomson Publishing Ltd
www.wtpub.co.uk
+44 (0)843 208 7460

Editor: Katie Dicker
Designer: Amy Sparks
Picture researcher: Katie Dicker
Series consultant: Kate Ruttle
Design concept: Paul Cherrill

British Library Cataloguing in Publication Data
Dicker, Katie.
  My dad. -- (Popcorn)
  1. Father--Juvenile literature.
  2. Father and child--Juvenile literature.
  I. Title II. Series
  306.8'742-dc22

ISBN: 978 0 7502 6308 5

Wayland is a division of Hachette Children's Books,
an Hachette UK company.
www.hachette.co.uk

Printed and bound in China

Picture Credits: **Corbis:** Image Source 8/13/20, Inspirestock 12, Heide Benser 14; **Dreamstime:** Monkey Business Images 5/23, Valua Vitaly 4, Yevette Maurer 15; **Getty Images:** George Doyle 16; **iStockphoto:** Joshua Hodge Photography 19; **Photolibrary:** Creatas 7, LWA/Dann Tardif 9, Randy Faris 10, Indeed 18; **Shutterstock:** Monkey Business Images cover/1/17/21/22l, Dmitriy Shironosov 6/22r, Sean Prior 2/11/22m.

Every effort has been made to clear copyright. Should there be any inadvertent omission, please apply to the publisher for rectification.

Contents

What is a dad?

Your dad is the person who made you with your mum. He may live at home with you.

Your birth parents are the people who made you.

A dad can also be someone who isn't your birth dad. This dad may live with your mum and help to care for you.

Sophie lives with her dad, her mum and her brother, Michael.

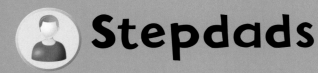

Stepdads

You have a stepdad if your birth mum marries someone who isn't your birth dad.

Molly's stepdad has looked after her since she was a little girl.

Theo has a birth dad and a stepdad. His stepdad, Ian, lives with him at home. His birth dad, Tony, lives an hour away.

Theo loves his birth dad and his stepdad in different ways.

Someone new

If your mum marries someone new, it can be difficult to get used to having another dad in your family.

Brett and Gina didn't know their stepdad well at first, but he was always looking out for them.

Talk to your parents about how you feel. They will understand that the changes might be hard for you to deal with.

Why do you think some people get married again?

Flo's mum and stepdad want Flo to be as happy as they are.

Working dads

Some dads go to work. They do this to earn money for all the things their family needs.

Amit's dad tries to have breakfast with his family before he goes to work.

Other dads stay at home.
Daniel's dad picks him up
from school before his mum
gets back from work.

Daniel and his
dad often make
dinner together.

11

Time together

If your dad works, he may
be tired when he gets home.
He may ask you to play with
him another time.

*How can you help
your dad when
he's feeling tired?*

Your dad would love to hear
about the things you've been doing.
Talk to your dad about the good
and bad things in your day.

Eva doesn't see her dad very often, but when she does, she tells him all her news.

Help and advice

Your dad has learnt a lot of things in his life. He's a good person to talk to if you need advice.

Ask your dad for help if something is bothering you.

Connor felt a lot happier when he told his dad how he was feeling.

Some dads can teach you new things. They can show you how to learn a new skill. Sarah's dad helps her to learn to swim.

Sarah feels safe in the water with her dad.

Working together

Sometimes, it's fun to help your dad when he's doing chores. You can talk and work at the same time.

William helps his dad with the dishes.

You can help your dad
with many things. It feels
good to help other people.

Suzie shows her dad where to
find the things they need to buy.

Understanding rules

It can sometimes be hard to get along with your dad. You may think your dad is being unfair.

Josh and Nadine have to brush their teeth to keep them healthy and strong.

Parents have rules because they want to keep you safe and healthy.

Talk to your dad about how you feel. You may find a way to make you both happy. This is called a compromise.

Callum's dad says he can go to James' house, if he's back in time for tea.

A special person

Learning how to get along with people is an important skill. If you and your dad get on well, it can bring you both a lot of happiness.

Your dad thinks of you even when you are apart.

Your dad is part of your family.
You care for him, and he
cares for you. This makes
him very special.

How do you like to spend time with your dad?

Dad time

1. Look at these photographs showing some of the children and their dads featured in this book. Can you answer these questions? Look back through the book if you need a reminder.

1. What does Suzie help her dad to do?

2. How is Molly related to her stepdad?

3. Why does Daniel's dad pick him up from school?

Answers: 1. Suzie helps her dad to find the things they need to buy at the shops. 2. Molly's stepdad is the man who married Molly's birth mum. 3. Daniel's dad picks him up from school because his mum is at work.

2. Here's a recipe you could make with your dad.

Egg and cress sandwiches

1. Put 2 eggs in a saucepan of cold water.
2. Bring the water to the boil and simmer for 10 minutes.
3. Ask your dad to drain the water and rinse the eggs in cold water until they're cool enough to touch.
4. Peel the eggs and put them in a small bowl. Use a fork to mash them up.
5. Add 1 tablespoon of mayonnaise and season with salt and pepper. Mix together well.
6. Butter 4 slices of bread. Divide the egg mixture between 2 of the slices and sprinkle with cress leaves.
7. Put the other 2 slices of bread on top and cut each sandwich. Enjoy!

Glossary

advice when someone helps another person with a problem they have

birth dad the man who made you with your birth mum

birth parents your birth mum and your birth dad

chores jobs that you do around the house, such as washing-up

compromise to find a way to make two people happy. Each person agrees to give up something in order to gain something else

deal to be able to handle a difficult situation

married when two people become husband and wife

stepdad someone who marries your birth mum (but is not your birth dad)

Index

Families

Contents of titles in the series:

WAYLAND